Fact Finders™

Biographies

Jesse Owens

Track-and-Field Champion

by Judy Monroe

Consultant:
Dr. Kenneth Goings, Professor and Chair
Department of African American and African Studies
The Ohio State University
Columbus, Ohio

Capstone press

Mankato, Minnesota

Fact Finders is published by Capstone Press,
151 Good Counsel Drive, P.O. Box 669, Mankato, Minnesota 56002.
www.capstonepress.com

Library of Congress Cataloging-in-Publication Data
Monroe, Judy.
   Jesse Owens: track-and-field champion / by Judy Monroe.
   p. cm.—(Fact finders. Biographies)
   Includes bibliographical references and index.
   ISBN 0-7368-3744-2 (hardcover)
   1. Owens, Jesse, 1913– —Juvenile literature. 2. Track and field athletes—United
States—Biography—Juvenile literature. I. Title. II. Series.
GV697.O9M66 2005
796.42'092—dc22   2004011216

Summary: A brief introduction to the life of Jesse Owens, the African American track star
   who won four gold medals in the 1936 Olympics.

Editorial Credits
Megan Schoeneberger, editor; Juliette Peters, set designer; Patrick D. Dentinger, book
   designer and illustrator; Kelly Garvin, photo researcher; Scott Thoms, photo editor

Photo Credits
AP/Wide World Photos, 16, 21
Corbis/Bettman, 4–5, 12, 15, 17, 18, 19, 22
Getty Images Inc./Hulton Archive, cover, 1, 13, 26, 27
Joyce Cole, 6–7, 8
Ohio State University Archives, 23, 24–25
Special Collections, Cleveland State University Library, 10–11

TM 2004 Jesse Owens by CMG Worldwide, Inc. / www.CMGWorldwide.com

1 2 3 4 5 6 10 09 08 07 06 05

Table of Contents

Chapter 1 Olympic Finals 4

Chapter 2 Childhood 6

Chapter 3 Cleveland 10

Chapter 4 Dreams Come True 14

Chapter 5 Home Again 20

Chapter 6 Olympic Legend 24

Fast Facts 27

Time Line 28

Glossary 30

Internet Sites 31

Read More 31

Index 32

Olympic Finals

Jesse Owens shook with fear. His first two Olympic qualifying jumps had failed. Now he was afraid he might step past the take-off board and foul. He had only one chance left.

Owens felt a hand on his shoulder. It was Lutz Long, Germany's star long jumper. He told Owens to start his jump a few steps early. That way, he wouldn't foul. Owens took Long's advice. He jumped far enough to make the finals.

In 1936, the Olympic Games were held in Berlin, Germany. At that time, Adolf Hitler ruled Germany. He believed Germans were better than people of any other race.

Jesse Owens flies through the air to win the long jump finals.

Hitler was shocked when Owens made the long jump finals. He was angry when Owens won the gold medal later that day. Hitler was furious that Owens, an African American, won four gold medals in Berlin.

Chapter 2

Childhood

James Cleveland Owens was born September 12, 1913, in Oakville, Alabama. His family called him J. C.

Owens was a sickly child. He had **pneumonia** nearly every winter. The family couldn't pay for a doctor. To help him recover, his mother, Emma, wrapped Owens in cotton sacks. She had him sleep in front of the fire. He slowly got better.

The Owens family was poor. Owens' father, Henry, was a **sharecropper** on a cotton field. His mother washed and ironed other people's clothing. Owens and his four sisters and five brothers helped in the fields. But the family earned very little money.

The Owens' house has been re-created at the Jesse Owens Museum in Oakville, Alabama. Visitors can learn about Owens' childhood.

Running

    After work, the children played games. Owens liked running games the best. He enjoyed running because it was something he could do all by himself. Running made Owens stronger. He soon noticed that he was faster than the other children.

Owens and his family ate dinner at a table like this one in the Jesse Owens Museum.

Owens' father also was a fast runner. After church on Sundays, the men in town held races. Henry Owens often won. Owens liked to watch his father run.

School

At age 6, Owens went to school. He and his brothers and sisters walked 9 miles (14 kilometers) to and from school. Owens often had to skip school. He had to help his family in the cotton fields.

Owens dreamed of going to college. He believed that college would help him become whatever he wanted. He wanted to do more than pick cotton all his life.

QUOTE

"We used to have a lot of fun. We never had any problems. We always ate."
—Jesse Owens

Chapter 3

Cleveland

When Owens was 9, his older sister Lillie was working in Cleveland, Ohio. The family decided to join her. They sold their mule and packed the few things they owned. The entire Owens family moved north.

In Cleveland, Owens was able to go to school every day. He went to Bolton Elementary School. At age 14, Owens started junior high school.

Coach Riley

Charles Riley coached the school's track team. He watched Owens run and jump in gym class. He asked Owens to join the track team.

Owens and his family lived in this house in Cleveland, Ohio.

By the time he reached
high school, Owens
▼ was a strong track star.

The track team practiced
after school. But Owens
couldn't practice then. He
had several afternoon jobs.
He shined shoes, delivered
groceries, and worked in a
greenhouse. Owens' family
needed the extra money.

Coach Riley agreed to
train with Owens before
school. Every morning,
Owens ran and jumped.
Riley taught Owens to run
smoothly and gracefully.

Setting Records

Owens quickly became
a track star. In 1928, he set
new records for junior
high **athletes**.

His success continued at East Technical High School. Riley was still his coach. In high school, Owens placed first in 75 out of 79 races. He set many high school records.

As a senior, he tied the world record of 9.4 seconds in the 100-yard dash. He also set a world record in the long jump. His jump was 24 feet 11.75 inches (7.6 meters).

13

Chapter 4

Dreams Come True

As a young child, Owens had dreamed of going to college. In 1933, that dream came true.

Many colleges wanted Owens to join their track teams. He chose Ohio State University. Owens worked three jobs to be able to pay for college.

Owens suffered the same poor treatment as other African Americans. In the 1930s, **segregation** separated whites from people of color. Owens could not live on campus with white students. African American athletes stayed in different hotels from their white teammates on the road.

Owens worked as a gas station attendant to earn money for college.

↑ Owens got along well with his track coach at Ohio State, Larry Snyder.

More New Records

Larry Snyder was Ohio State's track coach. He taught Owens how to get a faster start at races. He showed Owens how to kick in midair to get more distance on long jumps.

On May 25, 1935, Owens went to the Big Ten Championship in Ann Arbor, Michigan. In less than 45 minutes, he tied one world record and set three new ones. His long jump record of 26 feet 8.25 inches (8.1 meters) stood for 25 years.

To the Olympics

In early July 1936, Owens entered the Olympic trials. He won the 100-meter and 200-meter dashes and the long jump. His dream of competing in the Olympics came true. On July 15, Owens boarded a ship to sail to Germany. Nine days later, huge crowds cheered as Owens stepped off the ship.

Owens showed his skills to the other travelers aboard the ship to Germany.

17

Owens set an Olympic record in the 200-meter race.

Germany's leader, Adolf Hitler, was not happy to see Owens. Hitler believed that his German athletes were the best because they were white. He didn't want African Americans like Owens to win any events.

Owens wanted to win, and he did win. On August 3, Owens won his first gold medal. He ran the 100-meter dash in 10.3 seconds, tying the world record.

More Gold

Owens kept winning. On August 4, he set an Olympic record to win the long jump. His new German friend, Lutz Long, was the first to congratulate him.

Owens ran two more races. On August 5, he set an Olympic record in the 200-meter race. He earned another gold medal. Two days later, Owens led the American **relay** team to gold medals.

After the long jump, Owens and Lutz Long (left) watched the Olympics together.

QUOTE

"You can melt down all the medals and cups I have and they wouldn't be a plating on the 24-karat friendship I felt for Lutz Long at that moment."

—Jesse Owens

Chapter 5

Home Again

After the Olympics, Owens sailed back to America. Americans cheered for their new hero. They welcomed him with a huge parade in New York City.

At first, rich businesspeople offered Owens many good jobs. Owens was sure he would become rich. One by one, the jobs disappeared. Owens soon saw that white businesses did not want to hire an African American.

At the Olympics, Owens had shown that skin color was not important. But in America, skin color was still a challenge. Owens couldn't ride in the front of buses. He could use only the back doors of hotels. And he couldn't find a job.

Owens waves to the crowd welcoming him in New York City after the Olympics.

Looking for Money

Owens quit college to look for work. He had married Ruth Solomon in 1935. They had three daughters. Earning money for his family was important.

Owens tried to find new ways to make money. For a while, he ran races against horses. He won every time. But being treated like an animal hurt his pride. He quit the job.

Owens tried other jobs. He was a janitor, a bandleader, and a playground supervisor. He also opened the Jesse Owens Dry Cleaning Company. The business was unsuccessful and closed.

QUOTE

"People said it was degrading for an Olympic champion to run against a horse, but what was I supposed to do?"
—Jesse Owens

Finding His Place

Owens also gave talks. He spoke on the radio, at ball games, and to small groups. He was a good speaker. He told stories about his life and made people laugh.

In 1949, Owens and his family moved to Chicago, Illinois. The next year, sportswriters named Owens the greatest track star in history. Many people wanted to hire him. He now had plenty of work all over the country. Owens talked on TV, on radio, and in person. He started his own company giving speeches.

Owens gives a speech to soldiers at a military training camp.

23

Olympic Legend

Owens spent the rest of his life helping others. He especially liked working with kids. Owens headed the Chicago Boys' Club. He was head of the Illinois youth sports program. Over time, Owens started many new sports programs for kids.

Owens earned many **awards**. In 1976, he went to the White House to receive the Medal of Freedom. Three years later, President Jimmy Carter gave Owens the Living Legends Award. President Carter said Owens helped others reach for greatness.

"We all have dreams. But in
order to make dreams into
reality, it takes an awful lot
of determination, dedication,
self-discipline, and effort."
                    —Jesse Owens

Owens sometimes gave
swimming lessons to children.

25

↑ In 1965, Owens looked back on his success while visiting the site of the 1936 Olympics in Berlin.

FACT!

In his later years, Owens ran 2 miles (3.2 kilometers) every day. He also swam and lifted weights.

The Finish Line

In December 1979, Owens learned that he had lung cancer. In the early morning hours on March 31, 1980, Owens died. His wife, Ruth, was by his side.

Owens has not been forgotten. In 1982, Germans named a Berlin street leading to the Olympic stadium after Owens. His wife and three daughters helped to form the Jesse Owens Foundation. It gives college **scholarships** to deserving students. Most of all, Owens is remembered as a champion on and off the track field.

Fast Facts

Full name: James Cleveland Owens

Birth: September 12, 1913

Death: March 31, 1980

Hometown: Oakville, Alabama

Parents: Henry and Emma Owens

Siblings: Four sisters, five brothers

Wife: Ruth Solomon Owens

Daughters: Gloria, Beverly, Marlene

Education: East Technical High School in Cleveland; Ohio State University; received honorary degree from Ohio State University in 1972

Achievements:

Set many Olympic and world records

Four gold medals at the 1936 Olympics

United States Medal of Freedom, 1976

Living Legends Award, 1979

Time Line

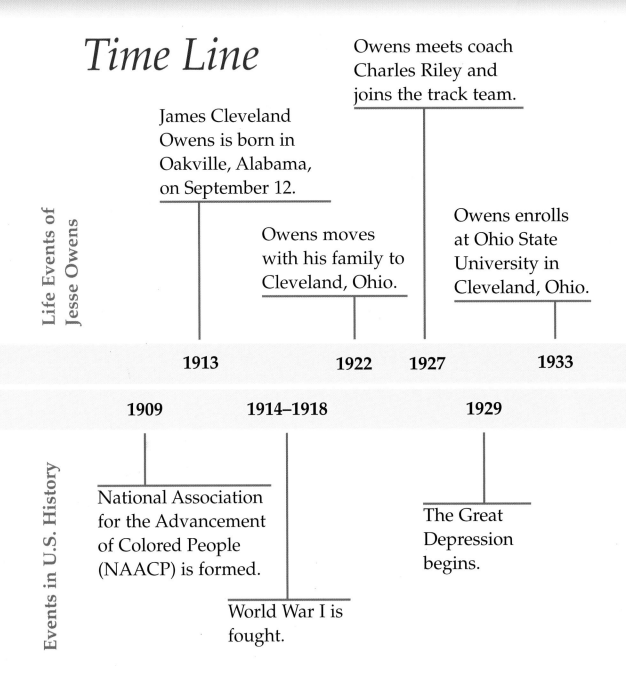

Life Events of Jesse Owens

James Cleveland Owens is born in Oakville, Alabama, on September 12.

Owens meets coach Charles Riley and joins the track team.

Owens moves with his family to Cleveland, Ohio.

Owens enrolls at Ohio State University in Cleveland, Ohio.

1913   1922   1927   1933

1909   1914–1918   1929

Events in U.S. History

National Association for the Advancement of Colored People (NAACP) is formed.

World War I is fought.

The Great Depression begins.

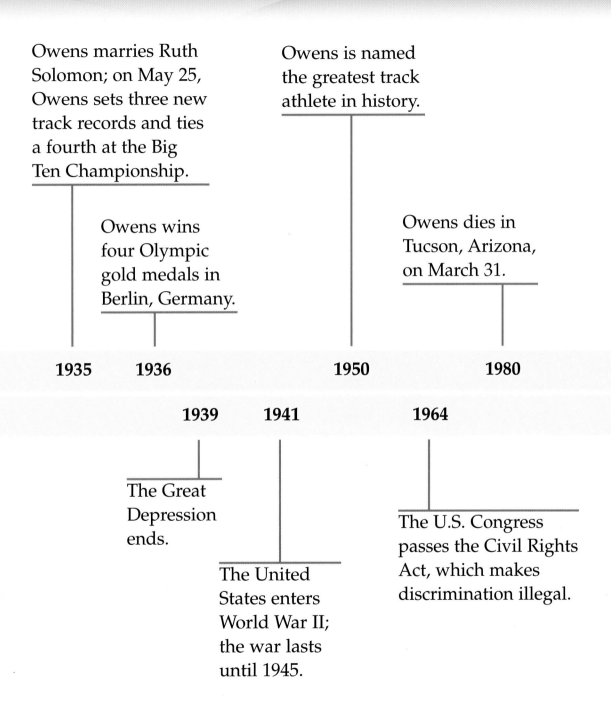

Owens marries Ruth Solomon; on May 25, Owens sets three new track records and ties a fourth at the Big Ten Championship.

Owens is named the greatest track athlete in history.

Owens wins four Olympic gold medals in Berlin, Germany.

Owens dies in Tucson, Arizona, on March 31.

1935   1936   1950   1980

1939   1941   1964

The Great Depression ends.

The United States enters World War II; the war lasts until 1945.

The U.S. Congress passes the Civil Rights Act, which makes discrimination illegal.

Glossary

athlete (ATH-leet)—someone who is trained in or very good at a sport or game that requires strength, speed, or skill

award (uh-WORD)—an honor or prize

pneumonia (noo-MOH-nyuh)—a serious disease that causes the lungs to become inflamed and filled with a thick fluid that makes breathing difficult

relay (REE-lay)—a team race in which members of the team take turns; in running relays, runners pass a baton from one runner to the next.

scholarship (SKOL-ur-ship)—a grant or prize that helps a student pay to go to college

segregation (seg-ruh-GAY-shuhn)—the act of keeping people or groups apart from one another

sharecropper (SHAIR-krop-ur)—a person who farms a piece of land and pays the owner of the land with money from the crops raised

Internet Sites

FactHound offers a safe, fun way to find Internet sites related to this book. All of the sites on FactHound have been researched by our staff.

Here's how:

1. Visit *www.facthound.com*
2. Type in this special code: **0736837442** for age-appropriate sites. Or enter a search word related to this book for a more general search.
3. Click on the **Fetch It** button.

FactHound will fetch the best sites for you!

Read More

McKissack, Pat, and Fredrick McKissack. *Jesse Owens: Olympic Star.* Great African Americans. Berkeley Heights, N.J.: Enslow, 2001.

Raatma, Lucia. *Jesse Owens: Track-and-Field Olympian.* Journey to Freedom. Chanhassen, Minn.: Child's World, 2004.

Sutcliffe, Jane. *Jesse Owens.* On My Own Biography. Minneapolis: Carolrhoda Books, 2001.

Index

African Americans, 5, 14,
    18, 20
awards, 24

Berlin, Germany, 4, 5, 26
Big Ten Championship, 16

Chicago, Illinois, 23, 24
Cleveland, Ohio, 10, 11, 12

Hitler, Adolf, 4–5, 18
horses, 22

Jesse Owens Dry Cleaning
    Company, 22
Jesse Owens Foundation, 26

long jump, 4, 5, 13, 16, 17, 19
Long, Lutz, 4, 19

medals, 5, 18, 19

Oakville, Alabama, 6, 7
Ohio State University, 14, 16

Olympics, 4–5, 17–18, 19, 20,
    21, 22, 26
Owens, Emma (mother), 6
Owens, Henry (father), 6, 9
Owens, Jesse
    birth of, 6
    childhood, 6, 7, 8–9, 10,
        12–13
    daughters, 21, 26
    death of, 26
    jobs, 12, 14, 20, 22, 23, 24, 25
    name, 6, 12
    school, 9, 10, 12, 13, 14,
        15, 21
Owens, Ruth Solomon (wife),
    21, 26

races, 13, 16, 17, 18, 19, 22
records, 12, 13, 16, 18, 19
Riley, Charles (coach), 10,
    12, 13

segregation, 14, 20
Snyder, Larry (coach), 16